To Patrick and Samuel—*B. K.*

To Seth—*P. H.*

Rabbit Ears Books is an imprint of Rabbit Ears Productions, Inc.
Published by Simon & Schuster, Inc.
1230 Avenue of the Americas
New York, New York 10020

Copyright © 1997 Rabbit Ears Productions, Inc.,
a subsidiary of Microleague Multimedia Inc.,
Lancaster, Pennsylvania.
Manufactured in the United States of America
10 9 8 7 6 5 4 3 2 1

Library of Congress Cataloging-in-Publication Data
Kessler, Brad.
Moses in Egypt / written by Brad Kessler ; illustrated by Phil Huling.
p. cm.
Summary: Tells how Moses grew up in the Egyptian pharaoh's court, was chosen by God to be
the leader of the enslaved Israelites, and called down plagues to convince the pharaoh to let the
Israelites go free.
ISBN 0-689-80226-9 (hardcover and CD)
1. Moses (Biblical leader)—Juvenile literature. 2. Bible. O.T.—Biography—Juvenile
literature. 3. Exodus, The—Juvenile literature. 4. Plagues of Egypt—Juvenile
literature. 5. Bible stories, English—O.T. Exodus. [1. Moses (Biblical leader) 2. Exodus, The.
3. Plagues of Egypt. 4. Bible stories—O.T.] I. Huling, Phil, ill. II. Title.
BS580.M6K44 1996
222'.1092—dc20
[B]   95-12493
                                                                                             CIP
                                                                                              AC

MOSES in EGYPT

Written by Brad Kessler   Illustrated by Phil Huling

Rabbit Ears Books

More than three thousand years ago, in the land of Egypt, a robust and handsome boy was born into the home of an Israelite man and woman. In a different time the child's parents would have rejoiced at the birth of a son. Yet at this time the Israelites were slaves in Egypt, and the king of the land—the pharaoh—had issued a terrible decree: that all boy babies born to the Israelites must be drowned in the Nile River.

Now God had led the Israelites to Egypt hundreds of years earlier when a great famine had ravaged their own land. And the man who was Pharaoh at that time gave them the best grazing land in all of Egypt, in a place called Goshen.

But when he died, new pharaohs came to power who feared the strength of the many Israelites and enslaved them. For a generation the Israelites were forced to labor under the burning sun as builders and bricklayers. And for a generation, they cried out to God and prayed for a liberator who would lead them out of Egypt.

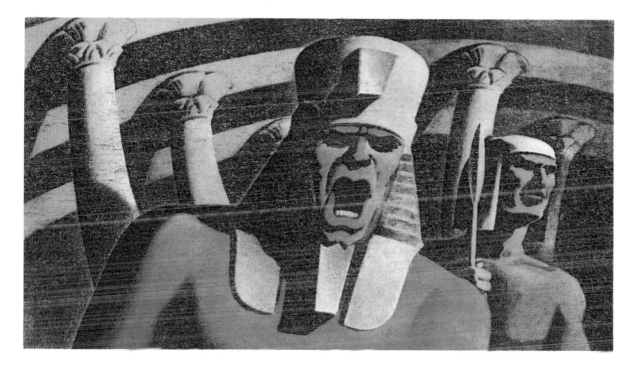

On that morning when the boy was born, Pharaoh's terrible decree had already taken effect, and the Israelites suffered more than ever. Yet this one woman resolved to save her son from Pharaoh's soldiers, for her heart would break from sorrow if harm were to come to the child. She hid the boy in her home for as long as she could—but after three months, she was unable to conceal him any longer.

So one night, while the whole city slept, she sat by the light of an oil lamp and wove together a basket of bulrushes and daubed it with pitch. And in the early morning, while the stars still shone in their places, she laid the boy in the basket and handed it to her daughter, Miriam.

Miriam ran to the place where Pharaoh's daughter, the princess, bathed each morning. She placed the basket among the bulrushes and hid behind a palm to see that the child would be safe.

As the mist rolled over the river, Pharaoh's daughter appeared on the bank. The first thing she saw was the basket among the reeds.

"Fetch me that basket," she said to one of her maidservants, who scurried down the bank and came back with the basket. The princess peered inside. "This must be an Israelite child!" she said.

Her voice wakened the sleeping boy, who began to cry, and Pharaoh's daughter took pity on him.

"I will take this child and raise him as my own," she announced. And because she took him from the Nile, she called him Moses, which means "drawn out of the water."

So the years went by and Moses grew up in Pharaoh's court surrounded by silk and sandalwood and roasts of meat and fine spices from the four corners of the land. He grew strong and tall and his tutors taught him to read and write and his bearers bathed him in lavender and rose water. Yet with time Moses came to know that while he lived in luxury, the Israelite slaves labored in the fields and were treated no better than beasts of burden by the Egyptians. And in his heart he was troubled.

One day, when Moses was a grown man, he went walking beside the brick pits where the Israelite slaves toiled. He saw his people, their mud-stained bodies bent and twisted from the weight of their bondage; he saw the agony in their faces and the welts on their backs from the lashes of their Egyptian masters. Finally, when he saw an overseer beating an Israelite, he could bear the injustice no longer. In a rage, Moses flung himself on the overseer and killed him. Then he buried the Egyptian in the sand and ran home.

The following day, Moses learned that many people knew of his crime and that Pharaoh sought to kill him. So Moses removed his silk robes and cloaked himself in a coarse wool garment. And that night, he fled Egypt on foot. He traveled by the dim trace of the moon, and for several days he walked alone through the hard wilderness of the Sinai. And when, finally, he reached the distant side of the desert, he felt safe, and rested there in a place called Midian.

So it happened that Moses made his home in Midian for seven years. During that time he became a shepherd and married a woman, Zipporah, and together they had a son named Gershom.

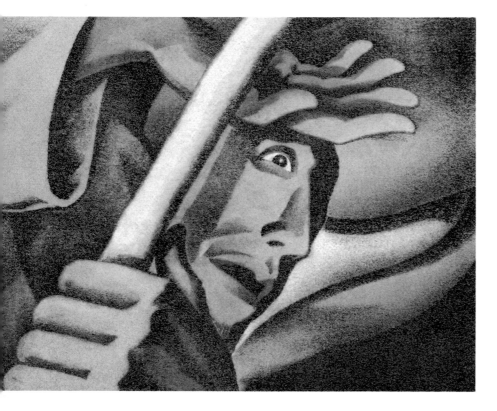

Early one evening, while he was leading his flock in the far west of the wilderness, he came upon Horeb, the mountain of God. And there he saw a green bush, blazing with fire. The bush crackled and leapt with flame, and the air glowed around it with a brilliant haze of red heat. But, miraculously, the bush did not burn.

As Moses drew near the bush, a voice as strong as ten thousand thunders boomed over the desert floor.

"Moses! Come no closer! Take off your sandals, for the place on which you stand is holy ground. I am the God of your father, the God of Abraham, the God of Isaac, and the God of Jacob."

Moses hid his face, for he was afraid to look upon God.

"I have remembered the covenant I made with your forefathers," God said. "And I have seen your people in Egypt. I have heard their cry and have come down to deliver them and bring them up to the Promised Land, a land that flows with milk and honey. It is you, Moses, whom I shall send to Pharaoh as my messenger; you who shall lead the Israelites as liberator out of Egypt."

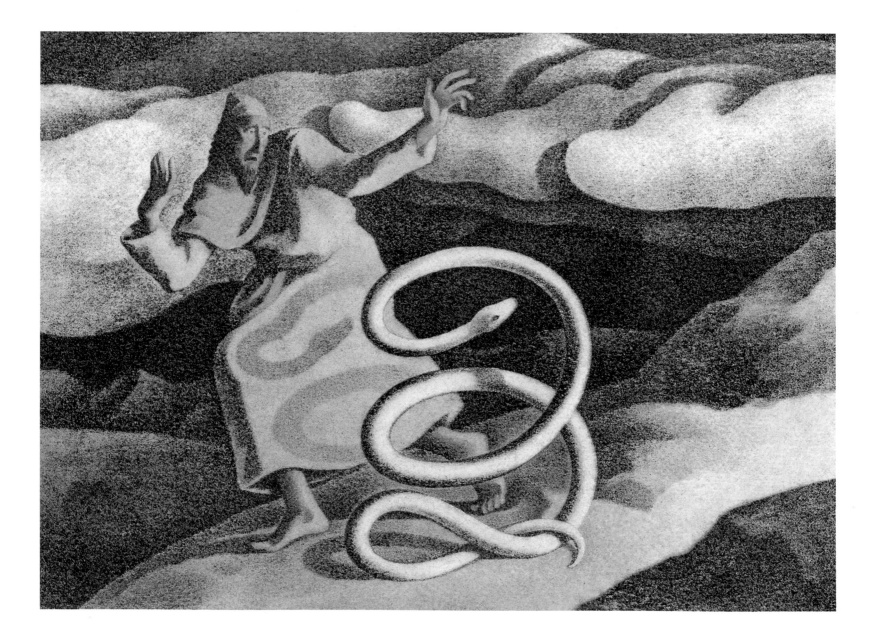

Moses could scarcely believe what he was hearing. "Who am I," he asked, "that I should challenge Pharaoh and lead the Israelites out of Egypt?"

"You shall not be alone," God said. "I will be with you."

Moses replied: "But what if I go to the Israelites and tell them the God of our fathers has sent me, and they ask 'Who is this God? What is his name?'"

"I am Yahweh," God said. "Say to the Israelite people, 'Yahweh has sent me to you.'"

"But Lord," Moses stammered, "they will not believe me or listen to me!"

"Cast your shepherd staff upon the ground," God said, and Moses did so. The moment his staff struck the ground, it was transformed into a serpent, and Moses leapt back in fear.

Then God told him to take the snake, and when Moses did, the serpent changed back into his shepherd staff.

"With that staff," God said, "they will believe the God of their ancestors has spoken to you."

"But Lord," Moses begged, "I'm slow in speech and I fear that no one will listen to me."

"Who makes a person swift or slow in speech, Moses? Is it not I, the Lord? I will be your eloquence. So go, Moses, for all those who sought you in Egypt are now dead and a new Pharaoh rules the land. Go, Moses, go down to Egypt."

With that, the fire in the bush died down and the hillsides fell silent again.

Moses departed from Midian and, with his wife and son, made the long journey back to his birthplace in Egypt. There he made himself known to his family and to his people, the Israelites, and when he told them of God's plans for their freedom and showed them the signs and powers God had given him, they bowed to him as their leader and spokesman. And then Moses went and stood before Pharaoh and his courtiers.

"The God of the Israelites has sent me," Moses said to Pharaoh. "And he has commanded me to tell you: Let my people go!"

Pharaoh sneered at Moses. "Who is this God of the Israelites? I know of no such God. I am the lord of this land."

With that, Moses took his shepherd staff and threw it to the ground. And before all the eyes of the court, the staff turned into a snake.

But Pharaoh summoned his sorcerers and magicians, and by their secret arts they did the same—each cast his staff into a serpent. Then, as they were laughing, Moses' serpent swallowed up the others. Yet Pharaoh was not impressed and ordered Moses away.

That night, Moses talked with God and God said: "Tomorrow morning, go to the Nile where Pharaoh bathes. Strike the river with your staff and the water will turn to blood. Tell Pharaoh, 'This is God's first plague, of which more will surely come unless you obey.'"

So the next morning, Moses did as God said. He rose early and went to the river and when he struck it with his staff, the waters turned bright red with blood.

But Pharaoh summoned his sorcerers and magicians. And by their secret arts, they too made blood from water, and Pharaoh ordered Moses away.

So after seven days, God sent down a plague of frogs over all of Egypt. The frogs flooded every field and market and every home and water well of the Egyptians.

Again Pharaoh summoned his sorcerers and magicians and, by their secret arts, they made their own frogs. And Pharaoh would not listen to Moses.

Yet after several days, when the frogs still covered the land, Pharaoh called for Moses.

"Tell your God to take away these frogs," Pharaoh said, "and I will give the Israelites their freedom."

The next day, all the frogs were cleared from the countryside. But just as soon as the frogs were removed, Pharaoh's heart became hardened and he went back on his word and refused to let the Israelites go.

So God sent down a third plague upon Egypt. And a great cloud of gnats rose from the clodded earth and crawled over the country and upon every Egyptian, young and old, rich and poor.

And Pharaoh summoned his sorcerers and magicians again, but this time they could not bring forth gnats from the earth with their secret arts. And they turned to Pharaoh in great fear and said, "Pharaoh, this is the finger of God!"

But Pharaoh would not listen and he sent them away. His heart was hardened and he refused to let the Israelites go.

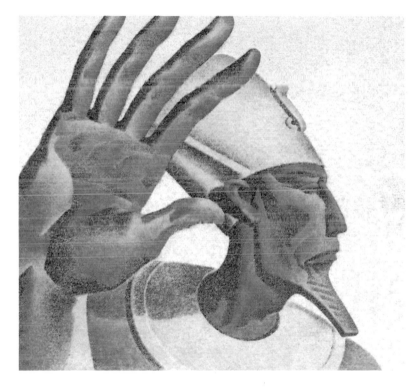

So God brought down six more plagues upon the land. A swarm of horse-
flies fell upon every Egyptian, from the simplest farmer to Pharaoh himself.
Then pestilence ravaged all the livestock and every cow and sheep and horse
died of disease. Boils broke out over the bodies of every Egyptian. Hail the size
of grinding stones fell from the heavens and smashed the homes and killed the
crops. A cloud of locusts covered the whole countryside. Then darkness

descended for three days all over Egypt—a darkness so thick not even fire could pierce it.

And each time Pharaoh begged Moses to stop the plague and said that he had been wrong before and promised, this time, he would let the Israelites go.

But each time Pharaoh's heart was hardened once more, and he would not let the Israelites go.

So Moses warned Pharaoh that his last chance had finally come—that the most terrible plague would fall upon Egypt. But as before, Pharaoh was proud and his heart was hard as stone.

That night, God spoke to Moses and said: "Yet one plague more I will bring upon Egypt. I will destroy the firstborn in the home of every Egyptian. And then Pharaoh will surely set you free. On the fourteenth day of this month, at twilight, every Israelite family shall slaughter a lamb. And they shall take the blood of the lamb and daub their doorposts with it. And this will be a sign for me to pass over the homes of the Israelites when I

destroy the first-born Egyptians. And hereafter, in every generation hence, this day you shall keep as a memorial to me, that I have passed over your homes and delivered you from slavery."

In the following days, Moses spread the word throughout the Israelite households. And when the appointed day came, the Israelites did what they had been told. They slaughtered lambs and marked their doorposts with blood.

And in the evening, they ate the lamb roasted with bitter herbs and unleavened bread. And they did so in haste, as God had commanded, with their sandals in place and their walking staffs in hand. Then they waited, as they had for many years, to be set free from Egypt.

At midnight, all of Egypt was quiet. Not a single cricket stirred in the fields, and the Nile slipped by silently in its banks. Then all at once, in the stone cities and out in the moonless towns, in the tents of the desert tribes and in the porticoed palaces of the nobles, in every home high and low, a cry shattered the night. For every firstborn Egyptian in the land had been killed, and there was no home that wasn't touched by death.

In his palace, Pharaoh too was awakened by the terrible screams. And when he saw that his own son was dead, he too became undone and his hard heart was pierced at last.

Pharaoh sent immediately for Moses. And when Moses arrived, Pharaoh was crumpled by his throne.

"Moses," he pleaded. "Rise up, go forth from Egypt, both you and the Israelites. Go serve your Lord and take your flocks and herds, and be gone!"

And with that, Moses went out into the streets and summoned the Israelites. And in the darkness before dawn, they took up their bread before it had time to rise and cast off their shackles and set forth from their homes.

And a great ragged column of them came forth from the Nile Valley—some six hundred thousand men and women and children and cattle and goats, with Moses marching at the head, holding his staff high in the air, for the hand of God had delivered his people from slavery.

And on the dark horizon, God created a great pillar of fire that swirled in the sky like a beacon, lighting their path from Egypt. And when the day broke, God created a pillar of cloud that rose before them like a great banner, leading them out.

And with a pillar of cloud by day and a pillar of fire by night, the Israelites went forth with a new song in their hearts.

Little did they know what hardships lay ahead, or how long it would take to get to the land promised them. But for a brief moment that day, it did not matter. They drank the cool draught of freedom; they inhaled the sweet smell, the succulent foretaste of the Promised Land. And on their tongues it tasted, that morning, of milk and honey.